POINTS: 12

WAM

636.16

P 26.93

3/22/2013

Marion School
410 Forest Hill Drive
Shelby, NC 28150

Designer Dogs

Chorkie

A Cross between a Chihuahua and a Yorkshire Terrier

by Sheila Hammer

Consultant:
Tanya Dewey, PhD
University of Michigan Museum of Zoology
Ann Arbor, Michigan

CAPSTONE PRESS
a capstone imprint

Snap Books are published by Capstone Press,
1710 Roe Crest Drive, North Mankato, Minnesota 56003.
www.capstonepub.com

Books published by Capstone Press are manufactured with paper
containing at least 10 percent post-consumer waste.

Library of Congress Cataloging-in-Publication Data
Cataloging-in-publication information is on file with the Library of Congress.
ISBN 978-1-4296-7669-4

Editorial Credits
Editor: Lori Shores
Designer: Veronica Correia
Media Researcher: Marcie Spence
Photo Stylist: Sarah Schuette
Studio Scheduler: Marcy Morin
Production Specialist: Kathy McColley

Photo Credits:
Ardea: Jeff Riedel, cover (top); Capstone Studio: Karon Dubke, cover (bottom right), 5, 7, 12, 13, 15, 17, 18, 19, 21, 22, 23, 25, 27,
    28, 29; Shutterstock: Claudia Naeredmann, 10, pixshots, 9, Utekhina Anna, cover (bottom left)

Printed in the United States of America in North Mankato, Minnesota.
112012   007021R

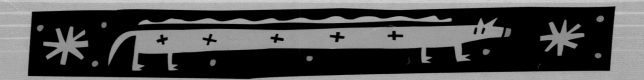

Table of Contents

Chapter 1

Silly Dog!

When it comes to cute and loveable dogs, few can compete with the silky and silly Chorkie. These little dogs may be short on size but not on charm. Chorkies are spunky and playful dogs. Many owners say their Chorkies are downright goofy. They love to play with toys and other small dogs. Some Chorkies even enjoy the company of cats!

There's more to Chorkies than their silly behavior, however. They're clever and curious dogs with a confident attitude. Chorkies have plenty of energy for playing, but they also make great lap dogs. They're affectionate pets that enjoy snuggling with their owners. Chorkies are brave but can be shy around strangers. Many Chorkies warm up to new people quickly. These **traits** make the Chorkie a popular designer dog.

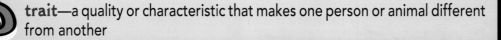

trait—a quality or characteristic that makes one person or animal different from another

4

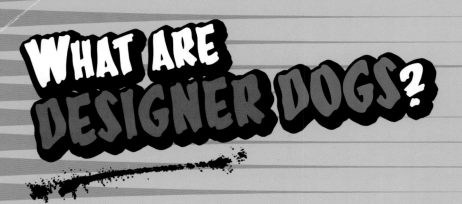

WHAT ARE DESIGNER DOGS?

A designer dog is a mix of two **breeds** of dogs. While designer dogs are not considered **purebreds**, they're not mutts either. Mutts are dogs that come from mixed-breed parents. Usually, the mix of dogs is an unplanned combination. Designer dogs are purposely bred from purebred parents to achieve desired traits. They're also called crossbreed dogs.

Sometimes dogs are bred for health reasons. Breeders hope that crossing two purebred dogs will prevent health problems common to the parent breeds. Other designer dogs are bred to avoid shedding. Some designer dogs, such as the Chorkie, are bred simply to be good pets.

breed—a certain kind of animal within an animal group; breed also means to mate and raise a certain kind of animal

purebred—having parents of the same breed

Join the Club!

The American Kennel Club (AKC), sets standards for the appearance and behavior of purebred dogs. Purebreds come from a long line of purebred dogs, so they should always look and act the same.

Designer dogs can have any mix of traits from their parents, however. They don't always look or behave the same way. For this reason, the AKC doesn't recognize designer dogs as purebreds, even though they have purebred parents.

A Jack-A-Bee is a mix of Jack Russell Terrier and Beagle.

Chapter 2

Mixing It Up

A Chorkie is a cross between a Chihuahua and a Yorkshire Terrier. To get to know the Chorkie, you need to know its parent breeds first. The traits of the parent breeds help predict a dog's look and behavior, whether designer dog or mutt.

CHIHUAHUAS

Chihuahuas are the smallest breed in the dog world. But what they lack in size, they make up for in personality. Chihuahuas are high-energy dogs that are always on alert. Their sharp barks quickly warn owners of trouble. These dogs also use their barks to let owners know they have visitors. They're loyal and devoted to their owners, so they can sometimes be aggressive toward strangers. If well **socialized**, however, Chihuahuas are friendly dogs that enjoy meeting new people. At home these tiny pups like to play and spend time with their human families.

socialize—to train to get along with people and other dogs

Chihuahuas are easy to recognize by their batlike ears. They all have large, pointy ears that stick straight up from their little heads. But the rest of their bodies can look very different from each other. Many Chihuahuas have short, smooth fur. Others have long, silky fur. Color combinations are almost endless. Common colors include tan and white. Their coats can be a solid color or have splashes of additional colors.

YORKSHIRE TERRIER

Yorkshire Terriers are also little dogs. Like Chihuahuas, they only weigh up to 7 pounds (3 kilograms.) They can be 6 to 9 inches (15 to 23 centimeters) tall. But unlike Chihuahuas, all Yorkies look similar. Their long, silky coats are always a combination of steel-blue and cream. Their long hair must be brushed every day to avoid getting **mats**. For this reason, many owners like to keep their Yorkie's coat trimmed short.

mat—a thick, tangled mess of hair

Yorkshire Terriers are popular pets due to their calm **temperament**. Yorkies are curious and playful dogs. Their terrier **instincts** make them brave and determined. But Yorkies are also sweet and friendly dogs that enjoy cuddles. They're devoted to their human families and seem happiest spending time at home.

Don't Play Too Rough!

Yorkshire Terriers, Chihuahuas, and Chorkies have plenty of energy for playing. But these small dogs can be easily injured if play gets too rough. When puppies play together, they yip to let each other know when a playful bite or scratch is too rough. But small children might not realize they're playing with their pets too roughly. For this reason, small breeds such Chorkies are not good choices for families with small children.

temperament—the combination of an animal's behavior and personality

instinct—behavior that is natural rather than learned

While Labradoodles and Cockapoos have been bred since the 1980s, Chorkies are new to the designer dog scene. Even so, these little dogs are a smash hit with people looking for cuddly companions. The Chihuahua-Yorkie mix gives the Chorkie a pleasant personality and appearance. Like their parents, Chorkies are energetic and playful. They're also brave dogs with bold attitudes. Some owners say Chorkies think they're big dogs.

Chorkies are usually built like their lean and athletic Chihuahua parent, though they still have some terrier features. Some Chorkies end up with longer legs than their parents. Most Chorkies' ears sit on top of their heads in triangles. Some Chorkies have little ears like Yorkies. Others have large, rounded ears like Chihuahuas. The fur on their ears can also be either smooth or fringed. Chorkies' coats can be one color or a mix of many colors, thanks to their Chihuahua parents. Their coats can be long or short with silky or coarse hair.

Mystery Puppies

   When Yorkshire Terrier puppies are born, their coloring is mainly black and tan. As they grow, their hair changes color to cream and steel-blue. Not all Chorkies will have amazing color-changing hair but some do. Chorkies that have the darker Yorkie coloring may develop lighter coats as they grow. Some Chorkies' coats even turn from black to gray with the change of seasons.

BARK, BARK, BARK!

Like both of their parents, Chorkies are confident dogs. But fearless natures and pint-sized bodies can sometimes spell trouble. Some Chorkies won't shy away from larger dogs. For Chorkies to be safe, they should be on a leash when outdoors. Chorkie courage can also lead them to leap off high furniture. Little dogs can be injured easily, so owners must take care that their Chorkies are playing safely.

Sometimes Chorkies' fearlessness can be an advantage. While Chorkies are too small to be guard dogs, they make excellent watchdogs. As loyal and devoted pets, Chorkies want to protect their owners. They are quick to bark when they sense trouble. They will also warn owners of approaching strangers. But owners say Chorkies don't bark as often as other small dogs.

Achoo!

Do dogs make you sneeze? Unfortunately for people with allergies, no dogs are completely **hypoallergenic**. People are usually allergic to an animal's dander. Dander is made up of flakes of dead skin that stick to the animal's fur. When the animal sheds, the dander is released causing allergic reactions. Fortunately for Chorkie owners, the non-shedding coat of the Yorkshire Terrier is usually passed on to Chorkies. And less shedding means less sneezing for many people.

hypoallergenic—possessing a quality that reduces or eliminates allergic reactions

Chapter 3

Chorkie Care

Chorkies are generally healthy dogs. With proper care, they can live up to 15 years. Like all dogs, Chorkies need to visit veterinarians regularly for checkups and **vaccinations**. Yearly checkups give the vet a chance to check for health problems. Chorkies can develop problems common to other small dogs, such as issues with their knees. Skin allergies and rashes are also common in Chorkies. If you notice that your Chorkie has itchy skin or a rash, talk to your vet. The vet can treat these skin problems so your pooch feels better in no time.

The vet also checks a dog's teeth. Small dogs often have dental problems. Brushing your Chorkie's teeth will help avoid these problems. The vet can show you how to brush your dog's teeth with toothpaste made for dogs. Some owners also offer treats that help clean dogs' teeth. Your vet will help you decide the best way to care for your Chorkie's teeth.

vaccination—a shot of medicine that protects animals from a disease

FEEDING TIME

Because Chorkies are small, you might think they don't need a lot of food. But these little dogs use lots of energy running and playing. A Chorkie should eat at least two small meals each day. Dog food made for small dogs will be easiest for their mouths. Your vet can help you determine what kind of food is best for your Chorkie and how much it should eat each day.

Danger: Little Dog Walking

Chorkies' cuteness comes from their little bodies. But those tiny bodies can be fragile. Little dogs running around underfoot might be accidentally stepped on or kicked. It's important to watch your step with a Chorkie in the house. An accidental kick can break a dog's bones or cause other injuries. Owners need to be careful to keep their miniature pets safe.

GET MOVING!

Exercise is good for everyone, and Chorkies are no exception. Even though they're small, Chorkies need lots of exercise to be happy and healthy. Chorkies don't tire easily, so they can run and play a long time. A Chorkie may still be up for a game of fetch even after a walk.

Without regular exercise, Chorkies can be overly active. Regular exercise will help them be calmer at home. But exercise isn't important just to burn off all that energy. Without enough exercise, small dogs can become overweight. Extra weight is hard on big dogs, but on little ones it can really affect their health.

The W-A-L-K

Daily walks are good exercise, but they offer your dog other benefits. Dogs have an instinct to walk with a **pack**. Walking with your dog helps strengthen your relationship. Walks also provide dogs with mental exercise. Dogs' sense of smell is more powerful than yours. Dogs pick up all sorts of new smells outdoors. The smells tell them information about other animals.

pack—a small group of animals that hunt together; dogs consider their human families to be their packs

GROOMING

Most Chorkies have short coats that don't shed much. Short coats need only occasional brushing. Chorkies with long coats should be brushed every day to keep the hair from tangling and forming mats. Hair around a Chorkie's eyes should be trimmed occasionally. If long hair interferes with the dog's vision or irritates the dog's eyes, it's too long.

The hair on a Chorkie's paws should be checked too. Hair that's too thick around the nails can cause trouble with walking and nail growth. It can be hard to keep some Chorkies still when grooming. With these dogs, its best to have a professional groomer trim their coats.

Most Chorkies need baths with dog shampoo every other week. Some Chorkies have slightly oily hair. Those dogs will need baths more often. Check your Chorkie's skin during bath time. Some Chorkies have skin allergies, so tell your veterinarian if you notice a rash. Check your Chorkie's nails too. After a bath, a dog's nails are softer and easier to trim. Have an adult trim your Chorkie's nails twice a month and use clippers made for dogs. Nails trimmed too short can bleed and be painful.

Training Time

Dogs need training to learn how to behave. After all, even you had to learn the rules of your house. The good news is that Chorkies are intelligent dogs that are easily trained. As devoted pets, they want to please their owners. Once they know what you expect, they will usually obey.

For Chorkies, rewards are a great way to help your dog learn. Start with basic **obedience training** such as sit and stay commands. These first commands will keep your pet safe and under control.

Offer small treats as rewards when the dog follows a command. You can also use praise, petting, and play as rewards. Just remember, the most important part of training a dog is you. Be patient with training and reward your dog for jobs well done. All your hard work will make for a happier dog and owner.

obedience training—teaching an animal to obey commands

Chapter 4

Is a Chorkie Right for You?

Chorkies make great pets for some families, but bringing a dog home is a big decision. If your family wants a dog, have a meeting to talk about it first. Adopting a dog is a big commitment. Can your family give it the care it needs? From grooming to vet visits and daily walks, a dog needs care from all members of the household.

Chorkies are loving dogs that become very attached to their human families. They do well with older kids but can be nervous around small children. Small children may also play too roughly with a little dog. Chorkies need companionship and attention to avoid getting bored and lonely. They don't like to be left alone for long periods. If your family is on the go much of the time, a Chorkie may not be the best fit.

Beware of Puppy Mills

Designer dogs are popular, but that's not always a good thing. Some people breed as many dogs as they can for profit. At these puppy mills, dogs are not given proper care. Puppies are raised in cramped, dirty spaces and often have health issues. If you decide to adopt a Chorkie, be sure to find a good breeder. Responsible breeders provide large, clean areas for their dogs. They will also show you proof that a puppy's parents are healthy.

TRAINING TIME

Chorkies do well in most places as long as they can get enough exercise. Unlike larger dogs, they fit well in small apartments. Chorkies also do well in houses with big families. Wherever you live, a Chorkie will be happy as long as its needs are met. A dog is a big responsibility. But with proper care, training, and love, a Chorkie can be a great family pet.

Should You Adopt a Chorkie?

Answer the following questions. The more "yes" answers you have, the more likely a Chorkie is right for your family.

1. Is someone home during the day to keep your dog company?
2. Does someone have time to walk and play with your dog every day?
3. Will there be time for daily brushing?
4. Do you have the patience to train a dog?
5. Will you be able to keep regular appointments with a veterinarian?

Glossary

breed (BREED)—a certain kind of animal within an animal group; breed also means to mate and raise a certain kind of animal

hypoallergenic (hye-poh-a-luhr-JEN-ik)—possessing a quality that reduces or eliminates allergic reactions

instinct (IN-stingkt)—behavior that is natural rather than learned

mat (MAT)—a thick, tangled mess of hair

obedience training (oh-BEE-dee-uhns TRAY-ning)—teaching an animal to obey commands

pack (PAK)—a small group of animals that hunt together; dogs consider their human family to be their pack

purebred (PYOOR-bred)—having parents of the same breed

socialize (SOH-shuh-lize)—to train to get along with people and other dogs

temperament (TEM-pur-uh-muhnt)—the combination of an animal's behavior and personality

trait (TRATE)—a quality or characteristic that makes one person or animal different from another

vaccination (vak-suh-NAY-shun)—a shot of medicine that protects animals from a disease

Read More

Gagne, Tammy. *Chihuahuas.* All about Dogs. Mankato, Minn.: Capstone Press, 2009.

Rosen, Michael J. *My Dog!: A Kids' Guide to Keeping a Happy and Healthy Pet.* New York: Workman Pub., 2011.

Schwartz, Heather E. *Morkie: A Cross between a Maltese and a Yorkshire Terrier.* Designer Dogs. Mankato, Minn.: Capstone Press, 2012.

Internet Sites

FactHound offers a safe, fun way to find Internet sites related to this book. All of the sites on FactHound have been researched by our staff.

Here's all you do:

Visit *www.facthound.com*

Type in this code: 9781429676694

Index